UNDERSTANDING OCD FOR KIDS

A Kid's Guide To Understanding, Coping, And Thriving With Obsessive Compulsive Disorder

Barbara B. Recce

INTRODUCTION

Obsessive Compulsive Disorder, or OCD, is a mental health condition that affects millions of people around the world. It is a disorder characterized by uncontrollable and intrusive thoughts, obsessions, and repetitive behaviors, or compulsions. OCD can be a challenging condition to live with, especially for children, who may not understand what is happening to them or know how to cope with their symptoms.

This book, "Understanding OCD for Kids," aims to provide children diagnosed with OCD and their parents with the knowledge and tools they need to manage and overcome their symptoms. It is an informative and comprehensive guide that explains what OCD is, how it affects children, and what can be done to help manage the symptoms.

Throughout this book, we will explore the various aspects of OCD, including its causes, symptoms, diagnosis, and treatment. We will delve into the science behind the disorder, and explore the different types of OCD that children can experience. We will also provide information on the different treatment options available, including Cognitive Behavioral Therapy, Exposure and Response Prevention, and medication.

But most importantly, this book is intended to offer hope to children with OCD and their families. We understand that living with OCD can be a challenging and often isolating experience. That's why we've included stories of children who have successfully overcome their OCD symptoms.

These stories serve as a reminder that with the right tools, resources, and support, recovery is possible.

One of the children whose life was transformed by the information in this book is Cole. Cole was an energetic and imaginative eight-year-old boy who loved spending his time exploring the outdoors and playing with his friends. But as he grew older, Cole began to experience intense, overwhelming feelings of anxiety and distress.

He would spend hours at a time checking and rechecking that his bedroom door was locked, washing his hands, and arranging his toys in a specific order.

Cole's parents were concerned and unsure how to help their son. They had heard of OCD, but didn't know much about it. That's when they stumbled upon **"Understanding OCD for Kids."** The book provided them with a clear and concise explanation of what OCD is and how it affects children. Armed with this knowledge, Cole's parents were able to seek out the help that their son needed.

With the support of his family and the guidance of a therapist trained in treating OCD, Cole was able to overcome his symptoms. He learned how to manage his anxiety and resist the compulsions that were holding him back. Cole's journey to recovery was not easy, but with the right tools and resources, he was able to regain control of his life.

We hope that this book will provide other children like Cole and their families with the same knowledge and resources that helped him recover. It is our goal to empower children and their families with the tools they need to manage their symptoms, live their lives to the fullest, and know that they are not alone in their struggles with OCD.

CHAPTER 1: WHAT IS OCD?

Obsessive-compulsive disorder (OCD) is a mental health condition that affects people of all ages, including children. It's a condition that causes people to have unwanted, intrusive thoughts or feelings (obsessions), and they feel the need to do something repeatedly to alleviate those thoughts or feelings (compulsions).

These obsessions are often unwanted and cause significant distress, and people with OCD feel like they cannot control them. For example, a child with OCD may have intrusive thoughts about germs or contamination and feel the need to wash their hands repeatedly to alleviate their anxiety.

Compulsions are repetitive behaviors or mental acts that a person feels they must do to reduce the anxiety caused by their obsessions. For example, a child with OCD may feel compelled to count to a certain number or touch things in a specific order.

While many people may have unwanted thoughts or feel the need to perform certain actions repeatedly, people with OCD have a harder time controlling these thoughts and behaviors. These obsessions and compulsions can take up a significant amount of time, affecting their daily life and ability to function normally.

It's important to note that having obsessions and compulsions does not necessarily mean a person has OCD. The diagnosis of OCD requires that these symptoms significantly interfere with the person's daily life and cause distress.

OCD can be a challenging condition for children to manage, and it's important for parents and caregivers to understand the condition and seek help if their child is showing symptoms of OCD.

It's also important to recognize that OCD is a treatable condition. With proper diagnosis and treatment, people with OCD can learn to manage their symptoms and live a fulfilling life. This may include therapy, medication, or a combination of both.

In conclusion, OCD is a condition that causes people to have unwanted, intrusive thoughts or feelings (obsessions), and they feel the need to do something repeatedly to alleviate those thoughts or feelings (compulsions).

While many people may have unwanted thoughts or feel the need to perform certain actions repeatedly, people with OCD have a harder time controlling these thoughts and behaviors. OCD is a treatable condition, and with proper diagnosis and treatment, people with OCD can learn to manage their symptoms and live a fulfilling life.

How Does OCD Affect Children?

Obsessive-Compulsive Disorder, or OCD, can affect anyone, including children. In fact, it's estimated that about 1-2% of children and adolescents have OCD. OCD is a mental health disorder that causes repetitive, unwanted thoughts or feelings, also known as obsessions, and repetitive behaviors or actions, known as compulsions. These obsessions and compulsions can interfere with a child's daily life and cause significant distress.

Children with OCD often experience a range of symptoms that can affect their behavior, emotions, and relationships with others. One of the most common symptoms is anxiety. Children with OCD often feel anxious about their obsessions or the need to perform certain compulsions. This anxiety can be overwhelming and interfere with their ability to participate in daily activities, such as going to school, playing with friends, or even just getting dressed in the morning.

In addition to anxiety, children with OCD may experience a range of other emotions, including sadness, anger, and frustration. They may feel embarrassed or ashamed of their compulsions or obsessions, which can lead to social isolation and difficulty making friends.

Children with OCD may also feel helpless or powerless to control their thoughts or behaviors, which can further exacerbate their anxiety and other negative emotions.

OCD can also have a significant impact on a child's behavior. Children with OCD may spend hours each day performing compulsive behaviors or rituals, such as checking and rechecking to make sure a door is locked, washing their hands repeatedly, or counting things. These behaviors can interfere with their ability to complete tasks, such as homework or chores, and can lead to frustration and difficulty concentrating.

OCD can also affect a child's relationships with family members and friends. Children with OCD may feel like they can't share their obsessions or compulsions with others because they fear judgment or rejection. They may become angry or defensive if someone tries to interrupt their compulsive behaviors, which can lead to conflict and strain in relationships.

In some cases, untreated OCD can lead to additional mental health issues, such as depression or anxiety disorders. Children with OCD may also be at increased risk for substance abuse or self-harm if they feel they can't control their thoughts or behaviors.

It's important to note that OCD is a treatable condition. With proper treatment, most children with OCD can learn to manage their symptoms and lead happy, healthy lives. Treatment may include a combination of therapy, medication, and self-help strategies. Parents and caregivers can play an important role in supporting their child's recovery by educating themselves about OCD, providing a supportive and understanding environment, and encouraging their child to seek treatment.

In conclusion, OCD can have a significant impact on a child's life, affecting their emotions, behaviors, and relationships with others. However, with proper treatment and support, most children with OCD can learn to manage their symptoms and lead happy, healthy lives. Parents and caregivers can play an important role in supporting their child's recovery by educating themselves about OCD, providing a supportive environment, and encouraging their child to seek treatment.

Why is it Important to Understand OCD?

Obsessive-compulsive disorder (OCD) is a mental health condition that affects people of all ages, including children. OCD is characterized by intrusive and distressing thoughts (obsessions) that are often followed by repetitive behaviors (compulsions) aimed at reducing the anxiety caused by these thoughts.

Understanding OCD is essential for both those who are affected by the disorder and those who support them.

Here are some of the reasons why it's important to understand OCD:

Early Detection and Treatment:

Understanding the signs and symptoms of OCD can help in early detection of the disorder in children. The earlier the disorder is detected, the easier it is to treat. Early treatment can help children learn to manage their symptoms and reduce the impact that OCD has on their lives. It also helps prevent the disorder from worsening and becoming more difficult to treat later on.

Reducing Stigma and Shame:

Many people with OCD experience shame and embarrassment about their symptoms. They may be afraid to seek help or talk about their experiences with others. Understanding OCD can help reduce stigma and promote awareness about the disorder, making it easier for people with OCD to seek help and support.

Improving Relationships:

Having a loved one with OCD can be challenging, and understanding the disorder can help improve relationships.

By understanding the symptoms of OCD, family members, friends, and teachers can offer support and help the child with OCD manage their symptoms. It also helps those around the child with OCD to be more patient, compassionate, and understanding.

Enhancing Treatment:

Understanding OCD can help enhance the effectiveness of treatment. It helps the therapist to tailor treatment to the individual needs of the child, making it more effective. By understanding OCD, parents and caregivers can also support their child's treatment and help them follow through with the treatment plan.

Promoting Self-Acceptance:

Understanding OCD can help people with the disorder to understand that their symptoms are not their fault. OCD is not a personal weakness or a character flaw, but a mental health condition. Understanding this can help those with OCD to accept themselves and reduce self-blame.

Empowering Those with OCD:

Understanding OCD can empower those with the disorder to take control of their symptoms. By understanding the triggers of OCD, they can learn to avoid or manage them. They can also learn strategies to cope with intrusive thoughts and manage their anxiety. This understanding can help them to take an active role in their recovery.

Understanding OCD is essential for both those who are affected by the disorder and those who support them. By understanding OCD, we can reduce stigma, promote early detection and treatment, enhance relationships, promote self-acceptance, and empower those with the disorder to take control of their symptoms.

CHAPTER 2: OCD BASICS

Obsessive-Compulsive Disorder (OCD) is a type of anxiety disorder that affects millions of people worldwide. OCD is characterized by repetitive, intrusive thoughts (obsessions) and compulsive behaviors or mental acts that are performed to relieve anxiety (compulsions). These thoughts and behaviors can be time-consuming, distressing, and may interfere with daily life activities.

Obsessive Compulsive Disorder (OCD) is a mental health disorder that affects people of all ages. It is characterized by unwanted, intrusive thoughts or feelings (obsessions) that cause anxiety and compulsive behaviors or actions that are performed to reduce this anxiety.

It is believed that OCD is caused by an imbalance in the brain's chemical and electrical signals, and understanding the brain is crucial to understanding this disorder.

The brain is a complex organ that is responsible for our thoughts, feelings, and behaviors. It is made up of billions of cells called neurons that communicate with each other through chemical and electrical signals. These signals are transmitted through the brain in circuits, or pathways, that are responsible for different functions such as memory, learning, and emotion.

One of the circuits in the brain that is thought to be involved in OCD is the cortico-striatal-thalamo-cortical (CSTC) circuit. This circuit connects different parts of the brain, including the prefrontal cortex, the basal ganglia, and the thalamus.

The prefrontal cortex is responsible for decision-making, problem-solving, and planning, while the basal ganglia is responsible for motor control and learning. The thalamus is a relay station that relays information from the sensory organs to the cortex.

In people with OCD, it is believed that there is an imbalance in the CSTC circuit, which causes the obsessions and compulsions associated with the disorder. Research has shown that there are differences in the structure and function of the brain in people with OCD compared to those without the disorder. For example, studies have shown that there is increased activity in the basal ganglia and decreased activity in the prefrontal cortex in people with OCD.

In addition to the CSTC circuit, other parts of the brain are also involved in OCD. The amygdala, which is responsible for processing emotions, is thought to be overactive in people with OCD. This can cause heightened anxiety and fear in response to certain triggers. The anterior cingulate cortex, which is responsible for regulating behavior and attention, is also thought to be involved in OCD.

Understanding the brain's involvement in OCD is important for treatment and management of the disorder. Cognitive Behavioral Therapy (CBT) and Exposure and Response Prevention (ERP) are two effective treatments for OCD that work by retraining the brain's response to triggers and reducing compulsive behaviors. Medications that affect the brain's chemistry, such as selective serotonin reuptake inhibitors (SSRIs), can also be used to manage OCD symptoms.

In conclusion, the brain is a complex organ that is involved in the development and management of OCD. The CSTC circuit, amygdala, and anterior cingulate cortex are all parts of the brain that are thought to be involved in OCD. Understanding the brain's involvement in OCD is important for developing effective treatments for the disorder and helping those who are affected by it.

Common OCD Symptoms in Children

Obsessive-Compulsive Disorder, or OCD, is a mental health condition that affects people of all ages, including children. OCD is characterized by the presence of obsessions, which are recurring and unwanted thoughts, and compulsions, which are repetitive behaviors or mental acts performed in response to these obsessions.

These symptoms can interfere with a child's daily life and cause significant distress.

Some of the most common OCD symptoms in children include:

Excessive cleaning and handwashing: Children with OCD may feel the need to clean themselves, objects or surfaces repeatedly. This can involve excessive handwashing, showering, or cleaning items in their surroundings. They may feel that they are contaminated or that germs will harm them or others.

Repeating behaviors: Children with OCD may feel the need to repeat certain behaviors, such as locking and unlocking doors, checking and rechecking homework, or counting objects. They may feel that repeating these behaviors will prevent harm from occurring to themselves or others.

Intrusive thoughts: Children with OCD may have unwanted and distressing thoughts that are difficult to control. These thoughts may be violent or sexual in nature, or involve harm coming to loved ones. Children may feel ashamed or guilty about these thoughts and may try to suppress them.

Order and symmetry: Some children with OCD may feel the need for things to be arranged in a specific order or pattern. They may spend hours arranging items or objects, such as toys or books, until they are symmetrical or "just right".

Fear of harm: Children with OCD may have irrational fears of causing harm to themselves or others. For example, they may fear that they will accidentally harm a family member or friend by not washing their hands enough, or that they will cause a fire by leaving a stove on.

Hoarding: Some children with OCD may have difficulty discarding items, even if they have no practical use or value. This can result in cluttered living spaces, which can cause distress to both the child and their family.

It is important to note that while these symptoms are common in children with OCD, not all children with OCD will experience the same symptoms. Additionally, symptoms can change over time and may worsen during times of stress or anxiety.

If you suspect that your child may have OCD, it is important to seek the help of a mental health professional. Treatment for OCD typically involves a combination of medication and therapy, such as Cognitive Behavioral Therapy (CBT) or Exposure and Response Prevention (ERP). With the right treatment, children with OCD can learn to manage their symptoms and live a fulfilling life.

Different Types of OCD

Obsessive-Compulsive Disorder (OCD) is a mental health disorder that can manifest in many different ways. It is characterized by intrusive and repetitive thoughts (obsessions) that cause significant anxiety or distress, and the urge to perform compulsions, which are repetitive behaviors or mental acts that are aimed at reducing the anxiety or preventing harm.

There are several types of OCD, each with its own unique set of obsessions and compulsions.

The most common types of OCD are discussed below:

Contamination OCD

Contamination OCD is characterized by an excessive fear of germs or other forms of contamination. People with this type of OCD may obsessively wash their hands, avoid public places, or constantly clean their surroundings. This type of OCD can be particularly challenging during pandemics or when living in environments with high levels of pollution.

Checking OCD

Checking OCD is characterized by persistent fears that something terrible will happen if a task is not completed correctly. People with this type of OCD may repeatedly check locks, appliances, or personal items to ensure that they are safe or functioning properly. This can lead to significant distress and may interfere with daily activities.

Symmetry and Orderliness OCD

Symmetry and Orderliness OCD is characterized by a strong need for order and symmetry in the environment. People with this type of OCD may feel the need to arrange items in a particular way or may become distressed when things are out of place. This can interfere with their ability to perform daily tasks, such as getting dressed or completing work assignments.

Hoarding OCD

Hoarding OCD is characterized by a persistent difficulty in discarding or parting with possessions, regardless of their actual value. People with this type of OCD may accumulate large amounts of clutter or refuse to throw away items that are no longer useful. This can lead to significant distress and may interfere with daily activities.

Intrusive Thoughts OCD

Intrusive Thoughts OCD is characterized by unwanted and intrusive thoughts that are often violent or sexual in nature.

People with this type of OCD may feel ashamed or guilty about their thoughts and may try to avoid situations that trigger them. This can lead to significant distress and may interfere with daily activities.

Sensory OCD

Sensory OCD is characterized by a heightened sensitivity to certain sensory stimuli, such as noise, texture, or temperature. People with this type of OCD may become distressed by certain sensations and may engage in compulsive behaviors to avoid them. This can interfere with their ability to perform daily tasks and may lead to social isolation.

Just-Right OCD

Just-Right OCD is characterized by a need for things to feel "just right." People with this type of OCD may repeatedly perform certain actions until they feel that they are completed perfectly. This can lead to significant distress and may interfere with daily activities.

It is important to note that people with OCD may experience symptoms from more than one type of OCD. Additionally, not everyone with OCD experiences the same symptoms, and the severity of symptoms can vary widely. It is important for individuals with OCD to receive proper treatment from a mental health professional who specializes in OCD. With the right treatment, people with OCD can learn to manage their symptoms and improve their quality of life.

CHAPTER 3: CAUSES AND TRIGGERS OF OCD

Obsessive-compulsive disorder (OCD) is a type of anxiety disorder that affects people of all ages, including children. It is characterized by intrusive thoughts and repetitive behaviors, often leading to significant distress and impairment in daily life. While the exact cause of OCD is still unknown, research has suggested that a combination of biological and environmental factors may contribute to the development of this condition.

Biological Factors

Biological factors are one of the key contributors to obsessive-compulsive disorder (OCD). Although the exact biological mechanisms behind OCD are not yet fully understood, there is evidence that suggests that several areas of the brain, as well as neurotransmitters and genes, are involved in the development of OCD.

The brain plays a critical role in the development of OCD. Research has found that several areas of the brain are implicated in OCD, including the orbitofrontal cortex, anterior cingulate cortex, and the basal ganglia. These areas of the brain are responsible for various functions, such as regulating emotional responses, decision-making, and movement.

The orbitofrontal cortex is responsible for processing information related to rewards and punishments. In people with OCD, this area of the brain seems to be overactive, causing them to assign too much importance to certain thoughts, images, or sensations, which can lead to compulsive behaviors.

The anterior cingulate cortex plays a role in regulating emotions and impulses. People with OCD tend to have overactive anterior cingulate cortices, which makes it difficult for them to suppress unwanted thoughts and urges.

The basal ganglia are a group of nuclei located deep within the brain, which are responsible for regulating movement and behavior. In people with OCD, abnormalities in the basal ganglia have been found to contribute to compulsive behaviors.

Neurotransmitters, which are chemicals that transmit signals in the brain, also play a role in the development of OCD. Research has found that serotonin, a neurotransmitter that regulates mood, anxiety, and impulse control, may be involved in the development of OCD. Low levels of serotonin are associated with an increased risk of developing OCD.

Genetic factors also play a role in the development of OCD. Studies have found that OCD tends to run in families, and that certain genes may be associated with an increased risk of developing OCD. However, genetic factors alone do not cause OCD. Instead, it is likely that a combination of genetic and environmental factors contribute to the development of OCD.

Overall, while the exact biological mechanisms behind OCD are not yet fully understood, there is strong evidence to suggest that several areas of the brain, neurotransmitters, and genes are involved in the development of OCD. Understanding these biological factors can help clinicians and researchers develop more effective treatments for OCD, and help individuals with OCD and their families understand the condition and its underlying causes.

Environmental Factors

Environmental factors can play a significant role in the development of obsessive-compulsive disorder (OCD) in children. These factors are external influences that can increase the likelihood of developing OCD or trigger its symptoms. Although OCD is primarily a genetic disorder, the environment can also have an impact on its onset and severity.

One environmental factor that can increase the likelihood of developing OCD is a traumatic experience. Traumatic events such as abuse, neglect, or witnessing violence can trigger OCD symptoms in children. Children who experience trauma may develop OCD as a way to cope with the traumatic event. For example, a child who witnesses a violent act may develop a fear of harm or contamination, leading to obsessive-compulsive behaviors such as excessive hand-washing or checking doors and windows repeatedly.

Another environmental factor that can increase the likelihood of developing OCD is stress. Stressful life events such as divorce, moving to a new place, or changing schools can trigger OCD symptoms in children. High levels of stress can also exacerbate existing OCD symptoms. Children with OCD may find it challenging to cope with changes in their environment, leading to increased anxiety and obsessive-compulsive behaviors.

Furthermore, parental behaviors can also influence the development and severity of OCD in children. Children of parents with OCD may have a higher risk of developing OCD due to genetic factors.

However, parents can also unintentionally reinforce obsessive-compulsive behaviors in their children by accommodating their OCD symptoms. For example, a parent who repeatedly checks the stove to ensure it is turned off may inadvertently teach their child to engage in similar behaviors, leading to the development of OCD.

Environmental factors can also impact the treatment of OCD in children. A supportive and understanding environment can help children manage their symptoms and achieve recovery. Children who have a positive support system at home and school are more likely to respond well to treatment. On the other hand, a stressful or unsupportive environment can make it challenging for children to manage their symptoms and may interfere with treatment.

In conclusion, environmental factors can play a significant role in the development and severity of OCD in children. Trauma, stress, parental behaviors, and the support system around the child are all environmental factors that can impact the onset and treatment of OCD.

It is essential for parents and caregivers to be aware of these factors and take steps to create a supportive environment that can help their child manage their symptoms and achieve recovery.

Triggers of OCD in Children

Obsessive Compulsive Disorder (OCD) is a mental health condition that is often characterized by intrusive, distressing, and repetitive thoughts or behaviors. OCD can affect people of all ages, including children.

In children, OCD can be particularly challenging as it can impact their academic, social, and emotional development. It is essential to understand the triggers of OCD in children to help parents and caregivers provide the necessary support and care for their children.

Triggers of OCD in Children are:

Biological Factors:

Research suggests that OCD may have a genetic component. Studies have shown that children with a family history of OCD are more likely to develop the condition themselves.

Additionally, children with OCD have been found to have differences in brain structure and function, particularly in areas of the brain that are responsible for decision-making, judgment, and impulse control. These biological factors can contribute to the development of OCD in children and may act as triggers for the condition.

Environmental Factors:

Environmental factors can also contribute to the development of OCD in children. Traumatic events, such as abuse or the death of a loved one, can trigger the onset of OCD in some children. Additionally, exposure to stressors such as academic pressure, family conflict, or social stress can exacerbate the symptoms of OCD in children.

Family Dynamics:

The family environment can also play a significant role in triggering OCD in children. Studies have shown that children who grow up in families with high levels of criticism or parental conflict may be more likely to develop OCD. Similarly, children who are excessively worried about their parents' well-being or have been conditioned to perform specific rituals or behaviors to keep their parents safe may develop OCD symptoms.

Perfectionism:

Perfectionism is a common trigger for OCD in children. Children who have high expectations for themselves or feel pressure to excel academically or socially may develop OCD symptoms. These symptoms can manifest as repeated checking, counting, or arranging behaviors that are related to a need for perfectionism.

Trauma:

Trauma can also trigger the onset of OCD in children. Children who have experienced traumatic events such as physical or emotional abuse, accidents, or medical procedures may develop OCD symptoms. Additionally, children who have witnessed traumatic events or have a history of anxiety or depression may be at a higher risk for developing OCD.

Conclusion:

OCD can be a challenging condition for children and their families. It is essential to understand the triggers of OCD in children to provide the necessary support and care for their children. Biological factors, environmental factors, family dynamics, perfectionism, and trauma can all contribute to the onset and exacerbation of OCD symptoms in children.

Understanding these triggers can help parents and caregivers develop effective strategies to support their children in managing their symptoms and achieving optimal mental health. If you suspect that your child may be struggling with OCD, seek professional help from a qualified mental health provider who can assess, diagnose, and treat your child's condition.

CHAPTER 4: DIAGNOSING OCD IN CHILDREN

Diagnosing OCD in children can be a complex and challenging process. It is important to understand that OCD is a mental health disorder that affects children and adults alike. It is characterized by recurrent and intrusive thoughts or images (obsessions) that are accompanied by repetitive and often ritualized behaviors (compulsions) that are aimed at reducing anxiety or preventing harm.

These obsessions and compulsions can significantly interfere with a child's daily life, academic performance, and social interactions.

Diagnosing OCD in children can be a complex and challenging process. It is important to understand that OCD is a mental health disorder that affects children and adults alike. It is characterized by recurrent and intrusive thoughts or images (obsessions) that are accompanied by repetitive and often ritualized behaviors (compulsions) that are aimed at reducing anxiety or preventing harm. These obsessions and compulsions can significantly interfere with a child's daily life, academic performance, and social interactions.

Signs and Symptoms of OCD in Children

Obsessive-compulsive disorder (OCD) is a mental health condition that affects people of all ages, including children. It is a type of anxiety disorder characterized by unwanted, intrusive thoughts and repetitive behaviors that are difficult to control.

OCD can be very distressing and can interfere with a child's daily activities, relationships, and academic performance. It is important to recognize the signs and symptoms of OCD so that children can receive the necessary support and treatment.

The signs and symptoms of OCD can vary widely from person to person, and even from one day to the next. In children, OCD can be particularly challenging to identify because some of the behaviors associated with the disorder, such as repetitive handwashing or checking, may seem like normal childhood quirks or habits. However, the severity, frequency, and duration of these behaviors are what distinguish them as OCD symptoms.

Here are some common signs and symptoms of OCD in children:

Obsessive Thoughts:

One of the hallmarks of OCD is the presence of obsessive thoughts, which are intrusive, unwanted, and persistent. These thoughts can be disturbing, frightening, or embarrassing, and they often involve themes such as contamination, harm, morality, or symmetry. Children with OCD may worry excessively about getting sick or dirty, being harmed, or doing something wrong, even if they know these thoughts are irrational or unlikely to happen.

Compulsive Behaviors:

In response to obsessive thoughts, children with OCD may engage in repetitive behaviors or mental rituals, also known as compulsions. These behaviors are aimed at reducing anxiety or preventing harm, but they are often excessive, time-consuming, and interfere with daily life.

Examples of compulsions in children with OCD may include repeatedly washing their hands, checking locks or appliances, counting or repeating words or phrases, or arranging objects in a certain order.

Avoidance:

Children with OCD may also try to avoid situations or stimuli that trigger their obsessions or compulsions. For example, a child who fears contamination may refuse to touch doorknobs or play with other children, while a child who worries about harm may avoid sharp objects or refuse to go outside. Avoidance can lead to social isolation, academic difficulties, and worsen anxiety over time.

Emotional Distress:

OCD can be very distressing and overwhelming for children, who may feel ashamed, guilty, or hopeless about their symptoms. Children with OCD may become irritable, anxious, or depressed, and may have trouble sleeping, eating, or concentrating. They may also have physical symptoms such as headaches or stomachaches, which can be a sign of stress.

Interference with Daily Life:

The most significant sign of OCD in children is when their symptoms interfere with their daily life, such as schoolwork, social activities, or family relationships. Children with OCD may struggle to complete tasks on time, miss school days, or have difficulty making friends. They may also have conflict with family members or teachers over their behaviors, which can exacerbate their anxiety and stress.

It is important to note that not all children with OCD exhibit all of these symptoms, and that some symptoms may be more severe than others. OCD is a complex disorder that requires professional diagnosis and treatment. If you suspect that your child may have OCD, it is important to talk to a healthcare provider or mental health professional who can help you understand the signs and symptoms, and provide appropriate treatment options.

Diagnostic Process

Diagnosing OCD in children can be a complex process, as the symptoms of OCD can often be difficult to distinguish from normal childhood behaviors. OCD is a mental health disorder characterized by repetitive, unwanted thoughts or compulsive behaviors. It is essential to recognize the symptoms early and get appropriate treatment to prevent the condition from becoming severe.

The diagnostic process typically involves several steps. It starts with a thorough evaluation by a mental health professional, who will assess the child's behavior and symptoms. The evaluation will include a clinical interview with the child and parents to gather information about the child's history, symptoms, and family history of mental illness.

The clinician may also use questionnaires and other diagnostic tools to get a complete picture of the child's symptoms and how they impact their daily life.

To diagnose OCD in children, the clinician will use the Diagnostic and Statistical Manual of Mental Disorders (DSM-5). This manual provides a set of diagnostic criteria for OCD, which includes the presence of obsessions, compulsions, or both. The clinician will evaluate the child's symptoms against these criteria to determine if they meet the criteria for OCD.

It is important to note that OCD symptoms can vary greatly from child to child. Some children may have more severe symptoms than others, while others may only have mild symptoms. The diagnostic process must take into account the individual child's unique symptoms and experiences.

Misdiagnosis can also be a problem, as OCD symptoms can often be mistaken for other conditions such as ADHD, anxiety disorders, or depression. A trained clinician will be able to distinguish between these conditions and provide an accurate diagnosis.

It is important to involve parents and caregivers in the diagnostic process. They can provide valuable information about the child's behavior and help the clinician understand how the symptoms are impacting the child's daily life. Parents can also play an essential role in advocating for their child and ensuring that they receive appropriate treatment.

Once a diagnosis of OCD is made, the child can begin treatment. Treatment for OCD typically involves a combination of medication and therapy. Cognitive-behavioral therapy (CBT) is the most effective treatment for OCD in children. CBT teaches children to identify their obsessive thoughts and compulsive behaviors and learn coping strategies to manage them.

In conclusion, diagnosing OCD in children is a crucial first step in getting the appropriate treatment. The diagnostic process involves a thorough evaluation by a mental health professional and an assessment of the child's symptoms against the criteria in the DSM-5. Misdiagnosis can be a problem, so it is important to involve parents and caregivers in the process. With an accurate diagnosis, children can begin treatment and learn to manage their symptoms effectively.

Misconceptions About OCD:

Obsessive-Compulsive Disorder (OCD) is a complex mental health condition that affects millions of people worldwide, including children. Unfortunately, there are many misconceptions about OCD that can prevent children and adults from seeking the appropriate help they need.

In this chapter, we will discuss some of the most common misconceptions about OCD and why they are untrue.

Misconception #1: OCD is just a quirk or a habit

One of the biggest misconceptions about OCD is that it is just a quirk or a habit that people can easily control. This is far from the truth. OCD is a serious mental health disorder that is characterized by intrusive, unwanted thoughts, feelings, or sensations, and repetitive behaviors or mental acts that the person feels compelled to perform.

These compulsions are not just simple habits that can be stopped at will. They are often time-consuming, distressing, and interfere with daily life. People with OCD may also experience anxiety, guilt, shame, or other negative emotions if they cannot perform their compulsions or if they fail to prevent their obsessions from happening.

Misconception #2: OCD is a result of bad parenting or personal weakness

Another common misconception about OCD is that it is caused by bad parenting or personal weakness. This is not true. OCD is a complex disorder that is caused by a combination of genetic, neurological, and environmental factors.

It is not a reflection of a person's character or upbringing. In fact, many people with OCD come from loving, supportive families and have no control over their symptoms.

Misconception #3: OCD is rare and only affects adults

OCD is not as rare as people may think. In fact, it is estimated that 1-2% of the population has OCD, and it can affect people of all ages, including children. While it is more commonly diagnosed in adults, it can also develop in childhood or adolescence.

Children with OCD may experience different symptoms than adults, such as excessive worry about contamination or harm, a need for symmetry or order, or a fear of making mistakes. It is important for parents and caregivers to be aware of these symptoms and seek help if their child is struggling.

Misconception #4: OCD is easy to diagnose and treat

Another common misconception about OCD is that it is easy to diagnose and treat. This is not always the case. OCD can be difficult to diagnose because it often co-occurs with other mental health conditions, such as anxiety, depression, or ADHD.

It also requires a comprehensive evaluation and assessment by a mental health professional who is trained in OCD.

Treatment for OCD can also be challenging because it often involves exposure and response prevention therapy, which can be uncomfortable and difficult for some people.

Misconception #5: OCD is a lifelong condition with no hope for recovery

While OCD is a chronic condition that requires ongoing management, it is not a lifelong sentence with no hope for recovery. With the appropriate treatment and support, many people with OCD can learn to manage their symptoms and improve their quality of life.

Treatment may include medication, therapy, self-help strategies, or a combination of these approaches. It may also involve support from family, friends, or peer groups.

Misconception #6: OCD is just about being clean or organized

One of the most common misconceptions about OCD is that it is just about being clean or organized. While some people with OCD may have obsessions and compulsions related to cleanliness or orderliness, OCD can also involve a wide range of other themes.

For example, some people with OCD may have obsessions related to harm or contamination, while others may have obsessions related to religion or morality. It is important to recognize that OCD can take many different forms, and not everyone with OCD will experience the same symptoms.

Misconception #7: Everyone has a little bit of OCD

Another common misconception about OCD is that everyone has a little bit of it. While it is true that many people experience occasional intrusive thoughts or compulsive behaviors, this is not the same as having OCD.

OCD is a diagnosable mental health condition that involves persistent, unwanted thoughts and repetitive behaviors that significantly interfere with daily life. It is not just a minor quirk or personality trait that everyone experiences.

Misconception #8: OCD is caused by traumatic events or experiences

Some people believe that OCD is caused by traumatic events or experiences, such as abuse or neglect. While traumatic experiences can certainly impact mental health, they are not the sole cause of OCD.

OCD is believed to be caused by a combination of genetic, neurological, and environmental factors, and it can develop in individuals with or without a history of trauma.

Misconception #9: OCD is a type of anxiety disorder

While OCD is often associated with anxiety, it is not technically classified as an anxiety disorder. Instead, OCD is categorized as an obsessive-compulsive and related disorder.

This is because the defining features of OCD are not just anxiety or worry, but rather intrusive, unwanted thoughts (obsessions) and repetitive behaviors or mental acts (compulsions).

Misconception #10: OCD is easy to overcome if you just try hard enough

Finally, some people believe that OCD is easy to overcome if you just try hard enough or have enough willpower. Unfortunately, this is not the case.

OCD is a complex mental health condition that requires specialized treatment and support. While self-help strategies can be helpful, they are often not enough to manage the symptoms of OCD on their own.

Treatment for OCD may involve therapy, medication, or a combination of approaches, and it may take time and patience to see improvement. It is important to seek professional help if you or your child is struggling with OCD.

CHAPTER 5: COPING WITH OCD

Coping with OCD can be challenging for both children and their parents, but there are effective strategies that can help manage symptoms and improve quality of life.

In this chapter, we will explore some of the most common coping strategies for OCD, including cognitive-behavioral therapy, exposure and response prevention, medications, and self-help strategies.

Cognitive-Behavioral Therapy

Cognitive-behavioral therapy (CBT) is a type of psychotherapy that has been shown to be effective in treating OCD in both adults and children. CBT involves helping the child to recognize their obsessive thoughts and compulsive behaviors and teaching them how to change their thought patterns and behaviors to reduce anxiety and improve their ability to function.

The therapist may use a variety of techniques, including relaxation training, cognitive restructuring, and exposure and response prevention, to help the child manage their symptoms.

One key aspect of CBT is exposure and response prevention (ERP). This technique involves gradually exposing the child to the things that trigger their OCD and helping them learn to resist the urge to perform their compulsions.

For example, if a child has a fear of contamination, the therapist may gradually expose them to situations that involve germs, such as touching a doorknob, and help them resist the urge to wash their hands. This process can be challenging, but with support and guidance from a trained therapist, children can learn to overcome their compulsions and reduce their anxiety.

Medications

In some cases, medication may be recommended to help manage OCD symptoms. Antidepressants, such as selective serotonin reuptake inhibitors (SSRIs), have been shown to be effective in reducing anxiety and compulsive behaviors in children with OCD. It is important to work closely with a doctor to determine the best medication and dosage for the child, as well as to monitor any potential side effects.

Self-Help Strategies

In addition to therapy and medication, there are self-help strategies that can be effective in managing OCD symptoms. One key strategy is to develop a daily routine that includes regular exercise, healthy eating, and good sleep habits. These habits can help reduce stress and anxiety and improve overall well-being.

Another important strategy is to practice mindfulness and relaxation techniques, such as deep breathing, meditation, and yoga. These techniques can help reduce anxiety and improve the ability to manage stress.

It can also be helpful for children with OCD to engage in activities that they enjoy and that give them a sense of accomplishment. This can help build self-esteem and reduce anxiety.

Support from Family and Friends

Finally, it is important for children with OCD to have the support of family and friends. Parents can help by learning as much as they can about OCD and working with their child's therapist to develop a treatment plan. They can also provide encouragement and support as their child works to overcome their compulsions and manage their symptoms.

It is also important for parents to be patient and understanding with their child. OCD can be a frustrating and challenging disorder, but with the right treatment and support, children can learn to manage their symptoms and lead happy, fulfilling lives.

CHAPTER 6: SUPPORTING A CHILD WITH OCD

Supporting a child with obsessive-compulsive disorder (OCD) can be challenging, but it is essential for their recovery. With proper support, children with OCD can learn to manage their symptoms and lead fulfilling lives. In this chapter, we will discuss how parents and caregivers can support a child with OCD.

How to talk to your child about OCD

If you suspect that your child has obsessive-compulsive disorder (OCD), it's important to have a conversation with them about it. Talking to your child about their OCD can help them understand their symptoms, reduce their anxiety and shame, and encourage them to seek treatment. However, starting the conversation can be difficult, especially if you're unsure of how to approach the topic. Here are some tips on how to talk to your child about OCD:

Educate yourself first

Before you talk to your child, it's important to educate yourself about OCD. Learn about the symptoms, causes, and treatments of OCD so you can speak confidently about the disorder. You can find information from reputable sources such as books, websites, or medical professionals. This will also help you understand what your child is going through and how to support them.

Find the right time and place

Choose a time and place where you and your child can have a private conversation without any distractions. Make sure your child is comfortable and not feeling rushed. It's also important to choose a time when both of you are calm and relaxed. Avoid talking about OCD during a stressful or busy time, like before school or before bedtime.

Be honest and straightforward

Start the conversation by being honest and straightforward with your child. Explain that you've noticed some behaviors or thoughts that are causing them distress and that you want to help. Let them know that they're not alone and that many other kids and adults have similar experiences. Use language that is age-appropriate and easy to understand.

Let your child know it's not their fault

It's important to reassure your child that their OCD is not their fault. Explain that OCD is a medical condition and that it's caused by a combination of genetic and environmental factors. Let them know that they did not cause it and that it's not something they can control or prevent.

Encourage questions and active listening

Encourage your child to ask questions and express their feelings. Active listening is an important part of this conversation. Listen to your child's concerns and acknowledge their feelings. Let them know that it's okay to feel anxious, sad, or scared, and that you're there to support them. Validate their feelings by saying things like, "I understand how you feel" or "That must be really hard."

Emphasize that treatment is available

Let your child know that there are effective treatments available for OCD. Explain that treatment can help them manage their symptoms and improve their quality of life. Discuss the different treatment options available, such as therapy or medication, and let them know that they can choose what works best for them.

Create a plan together

Create a plan with your child for managing their OCD. This can include strategies like practicing mindfulness or breathing exercises, setting goals for treatment, or identifying triggers and coping strategies. Encourage your child to take an active role in their treatment plan and let them know that you're there to support them.

End on a positive note

End the conversation on a positive note. Let your child know that you love and support them, and that you're proud of them for speaking up about their OCD. Encourage them to keep talking about their feelings and let them know that you're always available to listen and help.

Talking to your child about their OCD can be a difficult conversation, but it's an important one. By being honest, empathetic, and supportive, you can help your child understand their disorder, reduce their anxiety and shame, and encourage them to seek treatment. Remember to take the conversation at your child's pace, and to continue to support them throughout their journey.

How to Help Your Child Manage their Symptoms

Obsessive-Compulsive Disorder (OCD) is a type of anxiety disorder that causes intrusive, unwanted thoughts (obsessions) and repetitive, uncontrollable behaviors (compulsions). OCD can be challenging for anyone, but it can be particularly difficult for children who may struggle to understand what is happening to them or how to manage their symptoms. As a parent or caregiver of a child with OCD, it is essential to learn how to help your child manage their symptoms so that they can live a happy and healthy life.

Educate Yourself and Your Child

The first step in helping your child manage their OCD symptoms is to educate yourself and your child about OCD. You can start by explaining what OCD is in simple terms, and then providing age-appropriate information about how it affects your child. Be sure to emphasize that OCD is not their fault and that they are not alone in their struggles.

Create a Supportive Environment

It is crucial to create a supportive and understanding environment for your child. Avoid criticizing or belittling your child for their symptoms. Instead, try to be patient and offer encouragement when they make progress. Let your child know that you are there to support them throughout their journey.

Identify Triggers

Identifying triggers is an essential part of managing OCD symptoms. Triggers are situations or events that can cause an increase in obsessive thoughts and compulsive behaviors. Work with your child to identify triggers and then help them develop coping strategies for dealing with them. For example, if your child's trigger is a particular sound, help them find ways to reduce exposure to that sound or cope with it when it occurs.

Encourage Communication

Encouraging your child to communicate their thoughts and feelings is another important aspect of managing OCD symptoms. Create a safe space where your child can talk openly about their struggles without fear of judgment or criticism. Listen actively and provide validation and support.

Implement Relaxation Techniques

Teaching your child relaxation techniques can also help them manage their OCD symptoms. Deep breathing exercises, meditation, and yoga are all effective ways to reduce anxiety and stress. Encourage your child to practice relaxation techniques regularly to help them manage their symptoms.

Develop a Plan for Challenging Situations

Challenging situations, such as school exams or social events, can be particularly challenging for children with OCD. Work with your child to develop a plan for managing these situations. For example, if your child struggles with contamination OCD, develop a plan for how to manage their fears while in public restrooms or other potentially triggering situations.

Reward Positive Behavior

Finally, it is important to reward positive behavior. Celebrate your child's victories, no matter how small they may seem. Positive reinforcement can be a powerful motivator for children with OCD, and it can help them stay on track in their recovery journey.

In conclusion, helping your child manage their OCD symptoms requires patience, understanding, and a willingness to learn. By educating yourself and your child, creating a supportive environment, identifying triggers, encouraging communication, implementing relaxation techniques, developing a plan for challenging situations, and rewarding positive behavior, you can help your child live a happy and healthy life despite their OCD.

Remember, recovery is a journey, not a destination, and progress takes time. Be patient, and continue to support your child every step of the way.

How to Support Your Child in their Recovery

Having a child with OCD can be challenging, but there are many ways you can support them in their recovery. Recovery from OCD is possible, but it can take time, effort, and patience. In this section, we'll discuss some practical strategies for how to support your child in their recovery from OCD.

Educate Yourself

The first step in supporting your child's recovery from OCD is to educate yourself about the disorder. Learn about the different types of OCD, common symptoms, and treatments. Understanding OCD can help you provide appropriate support to your child, and it can also help you identify potential triggers and behaviors to look out for.

Be Patient

Recovery from OCD is a gradual process, and it can take time. As a parent, it's important to be patient and supportive of your child throughout their recovery journey. Avoid putting pressure on your child to get better quickly, and instead, focus on progress over time. Celebrate the small victories and be there for your child during the setbacks.

Create a Supportive Environment

Creating a supportive environment at home can also aid in your child's recovery from OCD. This means fostering an environment that encourages open communication, empathy, and understanding. Encourage your child to share their feelings and fears about their OCD, and let them know that they can talk to you about anything without judgment or criticism.

Encourage Treatment

Seeking treatment is an essential part of recovery from OCD. Treatment options may include cognitive-behavioral therapy, exposure and response prevention, and medication. Encourage your child to participate in their treatment plan, attend therapy sessions, and take medication as prescribed. Offer to accompany them to appointments and be involved in their treatment plan.

Practice Mindfulness and Relaxation Techniques

Mindfulness and relaxation techniques can be effective in managing anxiety and OCD symptoms. Encourage your child to practice mindfulness exercises such as deep breathing, progressive muscle relaxation, and guided imagery. These techniques can help your child learn to manage their anxiety and reduce the frequency and intensity of OCD symptoms.

Create Realistic Goals

Setting realistic goals is an important part of recovery from OCD. Help your child set achievable goals and celebrate their progress along the way. Encourage your child to focus on the positive changes they are making and remind them that recovery from OCD is possible.

Provide Positive Reinforcement

Positive reinforcement can be a powerful tool in supporting your child's recovery from OCD. Praise your child for their efforts and progress, and provide positive feedback when they exhibit healthy behaviors. This can help build their confidence and encourage them to continue working towards recovery.

In conclusion, supporting a child with OCD in their recovery journey can be challenging, but with patience, understanding, and support, it is possible. As a parent, you play a vital role in your child's recovery, so it's important to educate yourself about OCD, create a supportive environment, encourage treatment, practice mindfulness and relaxation techniques, set realistic goals, and provide positive reinforcement. Remember, recovery from OCD is possible, and with the right support, your child can overcome their symptoms and live a fulfilling life.

CHAPTER 7: LIVING WITH OCD

Living with OCD can be challenging, but with the right tools and support, it is possible to manage the symptoms and lead a fulfilling life.

Tips for living with OCD

Obsessive-Compulsive Disorder, or OCD, is a mental health condition that can cause significant distress and interfere with daily life. While there is no cure for OCD, there are ways to manage the symptoms and live a fulfilling life. In this chapter, we will discuss some tips for living with OCD.

Educate Yourself: The first step in living with OCD is to educate yourself about the condition. Learn about the different types of OCD and their symptoms. Understanding how OCD works can help you recognize when your symptoms are occurring and how to manage them.

Practice Mindfulness: Mindfulness is a technique that involves focusing on the present moment without judgment. It can be helpful for managing anxiety and intrusive thoughts associated with OCD. Mindfulness exercises can be as simple as taking a few deep breaths or practicing meditation.

Seek Support: Living with OCD can be challenging, and it's important to have a support system in place. This may include family, friends, or a therapist who understands OCD and can help you develop coping strategies.

Use Coping Strategies: Coping strategies can help you manage your OCD symptoms. Some common coping strategies include distraction techniques, such as listening to music or going for a walk, and exposure and response prevention (ERP), which involves gradually exposing yourself to anxiety-provoking situations and learning how to manage your anxiety in a healthy way.

Practice Self-Care: Taking care of your physical and mental health is essential when living with OCD. This includes getting enough sleep, eating a healthy diet, and engaging in regular exercise. Self-care can also involve participating in activities that bring you joy and reduce stress, such as reading, painting, or spending time with friends.

Set Realistic Goals: Living with OCD can make it challenging to accomplish tasks and achieve goals. Setting realistic goals that are broken down into smaller steps can help you manage your symptoms and feel a sense of accomplishment.

Challenge Negative Thoughts: OCD can cause negative thoughts and beliefs that can be difficult to overcome. Challenging these thoughts with evidence-based reasoning can help you manage your anxiety and improve your overall well-being.

Take Time for Yourself: Living with OCD can be overwhelming, and it's important to take time for yourself. This may involve taking a break from social situations or engaging in relaxing activities, such as taking a bath or reading a book.

In conclusion, living with OCD can be challenging, but it is possible to manage the symptoms and live a fulfilling life. By educating yourself, seeking support, using coping strategies, practicing self-care, setting realistic goals, challenging negative thoughts, and taking time for yourself, you can improve your overall well-being and manage your OCD symptoms. Remember, recovery is a process, and it's important to be patient and kind to yourself along the way.

How to Maintain Progress

Maintaining progress is a crucial part of managing OCD. Even after a child has completed treatment, they will still need to work on maintaining progress to prevent relapse. This chapter will cover several strategies that can help children with OCD maintain progress over time.

Stick to the treatment plan

The first step in maintaining progress is to stick to the treatment plan. If your child received cognitive-behavioral therapy (CBT) or exposure and response prevention (ERP) as part of their treatment, they should continue to use the strategies they learned in therapy. These strategies might include mindfulness, breathing exercises, or other coping techniques.

It is also essential to follow any medication regimen prescribed by your child's healthcare provider. If you notice any side effects or changes in your child's behavior, contact their provider right away.

Practice regular exposure

Exposure and response prevention (ERP) is an evidence-based treatment for OCD that involves gradually exposing a child to their feared situation or object while preventing them from engaging in compulsions. Exposure helps children confront their fears and teaches them that they can tolerate anxiety without engaging in compulsive behaviors.

Even after completing ERP in therapy, it is essential to continue practicing exposure regularly. This might involve continuing to expose your child to their feared situation or object at home, gradually increasing the intensity or duration of exposure as they become more comfortable.

Identify triggers

Another important strategy for maintaining progress is to identify triggers. Triggers are situations or events that can cause your child's OCD symptoms to flare up. Identifying triggers can help your child anticipate when they might need to use coping strategies and prepare accordingly.

For example, if your child's trigger is contamination, they might need to prepare for situations that involve being in a crowded public place or handling something that they perceive as dirty. Knowing their triggers can help your child prepare in advance and feel more in control of their symptoms.

Practice self-care

Self-care is crucial for maintaining progress. This might include getting enough sleep, eating a healthy diet, and engaging in regular physical activity. Practicing relaxation techniques, such as meditation or yoga, can also be helpful for managing stress and anxiety.

Encouraging your child to engage in activities they enjoy, such as sports or hobbies, can also be beneficial for their mental health. Having a support system, such as friends, family, or a therapist, can also be helpful for maintaining progress.

Celebrate successes

Finally, it is important to celebrate successes. OCD can be a challenging condition to manage, and progress can be slow. Celebrating small victories along the way can help your child stay motivated and feel proud of their progress.

This might involve setting small goals and celebrating when they are achieved. For example, if your child's OCD involves contamination fears, you might celebrate when they are able to touch something they perceive as dirty without immediately washing their hands.

Maintaining progress in OCD management requires ongoing effort and commitment. Sticking to the treatment plan, practicing regular exposure, identifying triggers, practicing self-care, and celebrating successes are all important strategies that can help your child maintain progress over time. With patience, persistence, and support, your child can learn to manage their OCD and live a fulfilling life.

CONCLUSION

Living with OCD can be challenging for children, but with the right resources, support, and treatment, it is possible for them to manage their symptoms and lead happy, fulfilling lives.

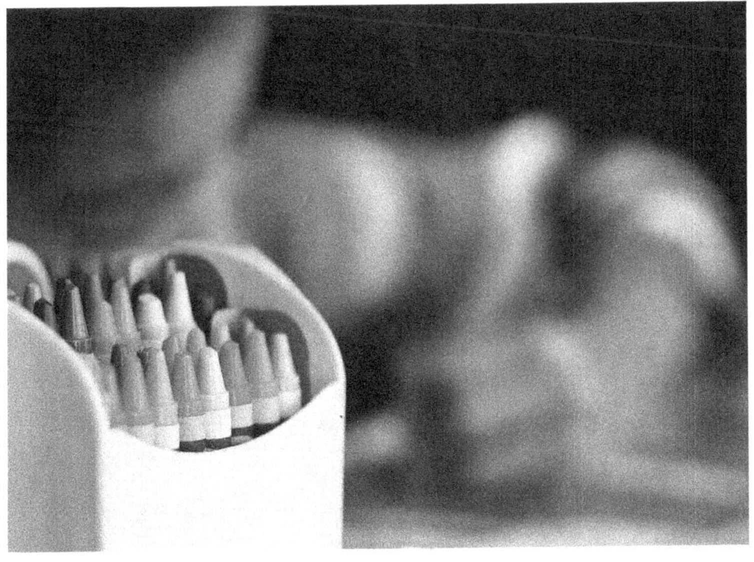

In this book, we have explored what OCD is, its causes and triggers, how it is diagnosed, and different treatment options available for children. We have also discussed how parents can support their children with OCD and how children can learn to cope with their symptoms.

It is important for parents, teachers, and caregivers to understand that OCD is a treatable condition, and with the right help, children with OCD can overcome their symptoms and lead successful lives.

Cognitive Behavioral Therapy (CBT) and Exposure and Response Prevention (ERP) are highly effective treatments for OCD in children, and they can help children learn to manage their symptoms and reduce the anxiety associated with OCD.

In addition to therapy, self-help strategies such as relaxation techniques, exercise, and journaling can also be helpful for children with OCD.

Parents and caregivers play an important role in supporting children with OCD. It is essential for them to provide a safe and non-judgmental environment for their children to express their feelings and concerns. They should also encourage their children to seek professional help if they suspect they have OCD symptoms.

Lastly, it is important to note that every child with OCD is unique, and their journey to recovery may be different from others. It is important for parents and caregivers to be patient and supportive, and to celebrate the progress their child makes, no matter how small it may seem.

In conclusion, understanding OCD is the first step towards helping children manage their symptoms and lead happy, fulfilling lives. With the right resources and support,

children with OCD can learn to cope with their symptoms
and achieve their full potential.

www.ingramcontent.com/pod-product-compliance
Lightning Source LLC
Chambersburg PA
CBHW061603250726
48657CB00017B/1777